OTHER ACREAGE

OTHER ACREAGE

BECCA J.R. LACHMAN

Gold Wake Press • Boston, MA

OTHER ACREAGE

ISBN 13: 978-0-692-32324-3

ISBN 10: 0692323244

Cover design by Brian Mihok

Interior Book Design by Christian J. Amondson

For my mom:

who wore a prayer covering to church,
a miniskirt to college, and—at age 60—
a divinity school graduation gown.

Contents

Preparation

Can we stop
holding
memorial services
for what
we did
not save?

Where
is the Wailing Wall
to grieve
for a set of fields
turned over?

What color
should a family
wear
to show a farm
is dead to them?

And why
did no one come
to take the keys
out
of a stranger's
hands?

Rumspringa

At secret slumber parties, Ruth and Ruby
burst out of back rooms
transformed. Their own version
of ascension: loosed
hair fanning pubic bones, they shrieked
louder than the rest of us. No bonnet, no
beckoning church. Strong legs
in borrowed Levi's,
our lipsticks strewn
through sleeping bags.

»»»

From stolen stacks of their brothers' outdated
films hoarded for *rumspringa*,
we watched *Insatiable*
Sandy and *Delilah Dives Deeper,* transfixed
and wondering how
much we really needed
to know, how we needed
to know our bodies. We tried

other worldly things (that most had tried
before us), convinced what we did cost
more: feathered bruises on thighs
and the pang of new words
later slapped from our faces. Tequila

and TP-ing the whole town
square, an innocent mess that fell in
soggy clumps by morning.

»»»

The "English" have no *rumspringa.*
Our testing of the world never ends.

»»»

Home on a visit, I see her
in the produce aisle: the New Order
Amish girl who once kissed me
hard. She has become
what the tourists mean to capture, looks back at me
as if studying art

that scares her. A baby silent
at her hip, another barefoot
and cloaked in the folds of her dress. I say her name
with a question mark. She smiles, looks away
from my city clothes and hair shorn down to
inches, my body medicined against
the threat of children. Her free arm reaches

for what is still needed; the other
firm, so practiced
at keeping in place
what she already has.

Figure 1.1 February 1, 65 degrees in SE Ohio. Our minds shift to "April" "earth," "skirts." We check lawns for daffodils in the making, our laundry remembering how to flap. No one checks the 10-day forecast. We don't want to know.

Let Me Feel, Dear Body.
Let Me, At Least, Desire

Too bad my people never bought
that *chakra* stuff. Our ladies' plain white caps
    could have been, instead, deep violet, asking
for the Spirit's charisma, His cerebral cortex
bliss. Communion bonnets? Green—center
    of the chest lit up with love's acceptance.
And when we held hymn sings, we might have slipped on
baby blue, our head coverings heart-shaped, the color
    of caution. No wonder friends tell me I look so
good in red these days, my blonde hair short
since writing my first real leaving
    poem. Look here: my closet's full of survival, not
the kind that left me gasping, but straddling exactly
what to wear, how much skin to show the world. O
    holy armor, please, *please* be orange: poppies'
warm lanterns led out from the grave each May.

Etymology

They want to be lifted,
my sister's children,
up to the oval
in the stall's shut door.

Whoa, they exclaim
at the cobwebbed
milking stations, then *Whoa!*
when another rusted

latch gives way: dim loft
and straw from our family
fields baled by a farmer
we don't know. I let them

run through dust and hay,
bury their hands in it,
fling it toward sunspots
on floorboards. What's left of

what we used to do here for
generations? They'll go home
covered with it. We'll walk
away, across the field, just

because it's easy. And we're
getting cold. And they want
to play somewhere new.

St. Francis Works at the Columbus Zoo

Does a soul really change
when we can't see its beginning? We pretend
we're in West Africa. Together,
we talk of rubber trees, how you miss the warm
throats of antelopes, a sun so hot the earth smells
of distant fires. We imagine our feet
calloused from heat, away from the patches of night-
silver snows in Ohio. Mostly, I'm here
to listen, then remind you of your role. Isn't that
what we all need from time to time,
for someone to notice, say, *Yes,*
you're living what you were made for?

Other workers play poker in the aquarium lobby
or sleep near the gift shop after feeding
the nocturnals. They only suspect me once the night
two high school boys dared each other to sneak into
the polar bear pool before dawn.
One boy's hand was already missing
by the time they all got there, having heard
the screams. I was already in the water, talking,
not to the boys, to the bears.

Tonight, the same bears are teaching two cubs
a creation myth, describe great walls of ice
that they will never see.
Remembering only a land of heat, you want to hear

this story too. So we follow winding sidewalks
to the other side of the world. Animals reach
beyond cages, tuck small flowers in your mane:
bush deer and elephant, pepper bird, baboon.

Cool cement beneath our feet, distant
highways for rivers, streetlamps for giraffes.
At night, I take off my shoes.

Twenty-four Crusts to be Frozen

SUNDAY: DAY OF REST

Rise when sky's amber. As coffee pot fusses, sift dry ingredients, butter the size of an egg. Measure out the needed doses. Have a passing thought about those years you weren't allowed in this farmhouse kitchen without permission, how your new mother-in-law clucked each time flour clouded to the floor, an accident. That was six decades ago. With first cup of coffee, toss a nimbus of the white stuff over both shoulders; show her who's boss. Use hands for blending, covering, fluting the shiny tins with dough—Like skin, you think each time you do it. Reinvent your body: so much promise, hundreds of new perfect fingerprints. Don't need an extra rib, just butter-flavored Crisco. Surgeries, babies; anniversaries, all those prodigal children. People need pies. You need them too, their soft empty faces, pastry crusts waiting for some soul to proclaim, "It is good. It is good. Best I ever had."

Figure 1.2 On my way to play piano for a ballet class, I spot a sunflower the size of my palm on the sidewalk ahead. *Escaped from a bouquet?* I think, excited, *Or a sign that spring's settled in?* I reach down to be its rescue—find out it's plastic. The rest of my day feels the same.

Bypass

My state doesn't believe in trains so I drive from one
person I love to another. Car passes farms, most
green fields snipped by giant scissors. Only
the heart of place remains: big house, proud
barn, a driveway shortened by lanes or filling
cul-de-sac, four-bedroom homes in the same muted
browns. I overtake a meandering
pickup just as my feistiest grandmother pushes out
all other thoughts, and I picture her for a few
seconds playing cards with friends still alive
or remembering. I race beyond a white barn with
turrets, another resembling a refrigerator box
left too long in the rain, then a barn with hinged
doors
missing, stalls stacked clear full with
harvest: unwanted plastic furniture, paint cans, the four
wheeler some son has been promising to fix
or sell. Their ancient paint, their patient
sturdiness
makes me think even more of my grandma's face,
then all those faces tucked away, letting someone else
look into them because we're busy, our day
planners full, sleep meds on the shopping list. (Listen,
there are things we just can't say without a phone.) *Stop*,
the barns bark at my rusting Toyota, at the semis strung
like rail cars beside me, and we

glance up, surprised. But we look away when
their decay feels sweet, too tender, too tied
to what took us a long time to shake.
And our molars start to hurt, and we forget to
exhale. Some of us
think "We'd be better off without such derelict
eyesores," especially next to a brand new
stretch of highway that gets us somewhere
six minutes faster. So we might speed
up just a little, maybe, Or maybe we keep
our eyes right on the road.

Joinery

Grandpa got to die in his own damn bed.
Eighty-some years of living, most in the same

set of rooms. After, dad stood in the John Deer's

ghost, gathered up a pile of barn pegs, extras,
everything standing without them. He brought me

two. My house is younger than I am. Here,

I paint a wall the color of earth turned over
after winter. Up north, some other family

will count triangle mud nests, catch kittens

on the silo's foundation, prime the pump to taste
our family's spring. At 102, my great-great-aunt

can still talk politics, though she's never registered

to vote. And she nods when I ask her if she was
born in *that house*. Like it isn't

so hard, after all, to start a slow walk

backwards. As if, like her, I can

already see it as someone else's

well-kept view

When Life Offers You a Grand Piano

you give away the downstairs furniture,
haul the couch up to the neighbors, half
apologize to guests and in-laws who must
now sit like hippies on floor cushions, cling
to kitchen table mere feet from beast
deserving of its lair.

You clean out your life for this ton-heavy
geode, this marooned whale shining
in your living room. You gut with gladness
all that's unnecessary

because what more is needed
than food and music, and why not mix
the two? You spicing curry while sonatas
spring into corners, measures played
by his hands that have memorized other

crescendos: the slope of your shoulders,
the weight of your breast. We wooed each other
with Chopin and Joni, the microphone
humid with breath, fingers knowing
all the high-stakes scales. It's a major chord

that will keep you both going, it's a breakfast
waltz that will ask you to be more
alive. Some days, you'll barely notice

how you've covered closed lid with junk mail
or newspapers, mittens and to-do lists—will forget
what that sleek back is really for. But did we know, before,

that a piano also has a cheek? Other days
your hand will linger there, follow rim until
it bends, pours open, makes
the shape of something hollowed
by the tides: in this room, a path
just wide enough
for two bodies to pass through.

Latest Letter

p.s.—Corn's shorter than usual this late into August.

p.s.—They've cut down the cedars along Nussbaum Rd.
Don't know how many locals have missed that turn!

p.s.—We're still refusing to get a stoplight.

p.s.—Your neighbor's draft horses nearly drowned in quicksand.
Took six men and two tractors, but they're fine.

p.s.—Your sister's little ones sure are growing! How long
have you been married now?

p.s.—If only you could see the sun at dusk
turn the white barns pink. The best silent movie.

p.s.—Your parents got caught at the recycling center
(It was night, there were *wine bottles.*)

p.s.—Six couples at church celebrating their 50th's. Now,
how long have you been married again?

p.s.—Remember how tar bubbles up on gravel roads?
Well, we're in the thick of it.

p.s.—That dead G.H owl in your daddy's plum orchard?
It's next in line at the taxidermist.

p.s.—What meats are you making for your company
at dinner? We just can't get enough
of your Grandma Ruth's ham balls!

p.s.— Thanks for the note last week. What do you mean
by "tofu" and "kefir"?

p.s.—They've changed 606 to 118 in the blue Mennonite hymnal.
There have been letters to the editor.

p.s.—*The Gazette's* weekly headline: "Pig Causes Traffic Accident."

p.s.—Your parents said 'no' to buying the farm.

(*How long* have you been married?)

p.s.—Hoods burned down the railway bridge
and your Grandma butchered chickens
on the clothesline this morning.

p.s.—We've got lots of starts for you: coneflowers,
daffodils, creeping phlox. So you can
plant something there and it keeps coming back—
even if it's in strange ground.

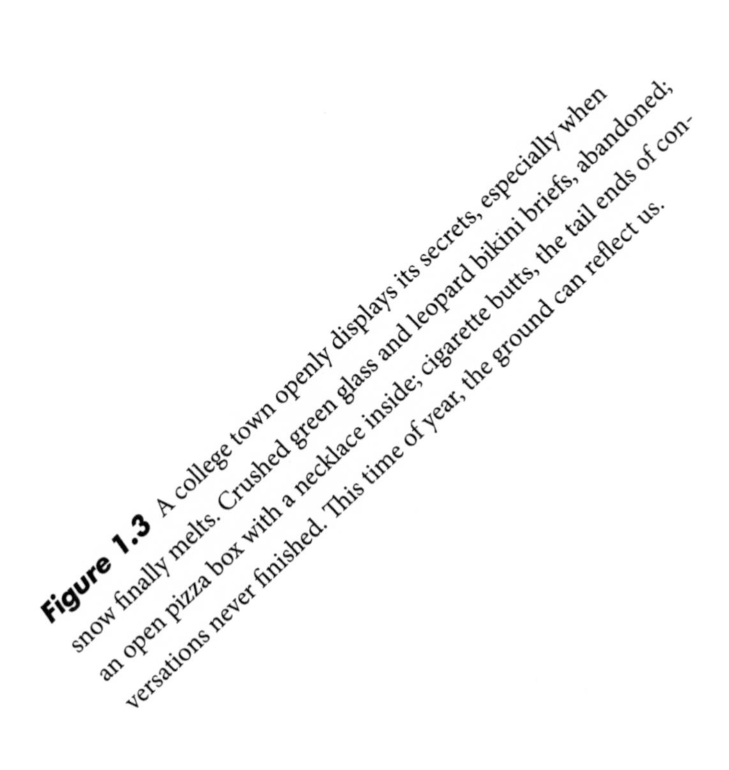

Figure 1.3 A college town openly displays its secrets, especially when snow finally melts. Crushed green glass and leopard bikini briefs, abandoned; an open pizza box with a necklace inside; cigarette butts, the tail ends of conversations never finished. This time of year, the ground can reflect us.

Someone Calls from the Porch, A High Voice Answers

THURSDAY: MUD PIE

Praise for what the farmhouse holds! Its crocks and icebox, its sewing room! The attic gluttonous with Grandma's thirty years of teaching: stuffed armadillo and spinning wheel, dead rattle snake in a pickle jar! Dear house, remain our source of story: hymn for white antique piano built right into the wall, for ancient Deepfreeze and mud-straw insulation, the first front door now painted shut. Praises be! for the steps where Grandpa led a pony to the best and cleanest bedroom, just to prove a *shuslich* could. Yes, praise for Swiss lowbrow, for psalms droned in German pressed into floorboards—our new feet hurry to another room. An ode to arrowheads untombed by the tiller, to buttons and china in the old family dump! Psalms to the scraps of the last generation our children polish for wild décor! In mud pies and castles, a bit of green gleams, squints an eye.

St. Francis Buys The Burrito Buggy

There comes a point when cleaving's just
necessary. Once started, the split in a map
leading home tears easy. So do bills
from a father's wallet. When money burns,
the smoke smells almost sweet. The only son, he leaves

with an old backpack, hitchhikes from Boston
to southern Ohio. He knows a guy there who's
selling a yellow food cart. He likes the idea
of farmland and a small room that's
rented. All his life, he's known
private schools and drivers. Better

to find out what's free and filling: pear trees
along a bike path or listening for hours
at the local mass, how it makes him feel like a shell
pressed to another's ear. Better to find
something small that keeps people happy,

then plunge in both hands: every day, a pan
of hot dish water, tubs of just-shredded lettuce,
the tip jar emptied into the hats of runaways. Tomatoes
are local, and the special's always the same: 4 *BUCKS*
FOR A GRANDE VEGGIE BURRITO. He keeps
his tortillas warm, just in case. Waiting
for their orders, bankers, pimps, grad students,

grandmothers admit all sorts of things. They want to be
better, have maybe had one beer or line too many,
and they don't need to know his name
or story, why the grumbling in his belly
never leaves. What they really want is comfort,

the next small step laid out. He can nod along
in empathy, listen for half an hour if need be. And he can
lean through the cracked sliding window to give them
something warm to unwrap, nothing
too mysterious.

No Photos, Please

Even now, this body belongs
to another world, another

empire claims it. By fist-
fulls, knead it back, ask daily

for its bending weight to wake,
arise. The light in each lung—

such flames will burn right
through. Yes, once you could,

you could look at us
and know what we were

using for a match. I might pass
you, and you'd take a photograph,

see my stolen soul ignite, a burn-
pile scrap filched by breezes,

curling in on three corners
just before its brightest pose.

Fence

No translucent moon-eye
caps for communion. My closet's full
of zippers. My own bread; white

wine in the cup, only—

look at my life: it knows the high
ways home. Some days I want
that plain mark too: an ankle-length

life, the unquest-

tioned difference
brought in off the line, starched
with dangerous iron—for others

to see what I've chosen.

He smiled, then scoffed, *you*
don't want a tattoo, you want a birth-
mark, lady when I picked

the ivy leaf— just an outline,

really. I didn't let him know
he was right: I couldn't run
forever, didn't even want to.

I'm still asking

for the gospel of my body to be
branded with some ever-
lasting faith, even just in ink.

Tourist Brochure For Athens, Ohio

Round here, breaded chicken hearts will cost you
    $2.50 a box.
Round here, upright pianos can end up on the porch (too
    expensive to tune, too bulky of an animal).
Round here, a squirrel could once tree itself in Parkersburg, end up
    in Indiana, and never
    touch the ground.
Round here, the pawpaw goes into homebrews, ice cream,
    salsas, even
    has its own fall festival.
Round here, there's no train out. Not any-
    more. Bus leaves for Cinci or Columbus.
Round here, the college lawns get unrivalled attention. No
    water or electric ten minutes down the road . . .
    Some folks play settlers, live that way on purpose.
Round here, we shine old mining towns into delis and
    meditation rooms. The last brick beehive kiln just
    got its first real crack.
Round here, student condos went up on Shawnee
    burial mounds. Their new front porches wear
    sloppy necklaces made from red party cups.
Round here, we got 270 cemeteries—some of 'em move.
    Just ask anybody up on Peach Ridge Rd.

Round here, ghost hunters stare right back at the crying
angel statue or the face of the devil on a door in
Wilson Hall. Spectral mist? We got it. Ghost herd
of bison? A big draw.
Round here, the old asylum closed some twenty years back. There's
movement behind windows. We find
a bit of lace out on the lawn.
Round here, you'd be committed for irregular bleeding,
post-traumatic fits, excessive
childbirth. Struck by lightning, even—in ya'd go.
Round here, still meet patients who came on down the hill
when all that funding went wonky in the '80s.
Round here, our children got two choices, mostly: get out,
or get in uniform. Creeks slip down the mountains,
orange ribbons full of acid. We already know
that story: "Little Cities of Black Diamonds."
We're workin' on a newer title, yeah we're workin'
pretty hard.
Round here, we say *Appalachia*
any way we damn well please.

Figure 1.4 For seven weeks, I gently build up to two questions, give my poetry students hard homework: What does it mean to be a writer in a time of war?, What would you ask a soldier, if you could ask him anything? Only half the class shows up to answer. I come home and pull covers up over my head, just another bulb.

All Day I Let the House

All day I let the house
be filled with voices
on the news. This morning, my body
forgives me
for this extra layer
of violence.

This morning, I leave the house
with a book
of half-read poems,
hold it beside me, my worry
stone.

St. Francis Appears at the Scene of an Accident, Then Joins the Murmuration

Black. Muscle. Stars. Wind.
The horse was nearly torn in half.
Black. Pulse. Strange. Light.
The car's right side was twisted open.
Black. Crust. Oil. Shine.

Imagine the night, the boy, the stallion,
all of them closing in, loose
for the first time in months. The car's pointed
hood, the horse's neck, a low
winter sky, farmland growing
houses in suburbia.

Lost. Happy. Speed. Speed.
Black-upon-Black-on-Black, and then—
Dirt. Muscle. Stars. Wind.
gravel leading to unfinished cul-de-sac.
Black. Pulse. Strange. Light.

There were stars, yes, eyes squinted in velvet,
and squares of sudden color, bedrooms lit
like match heads, fathers running to see
what made that noise,
that noise, to rush through doors
into daughters' bedrooms.

Black. Perfect. Revvv. Ready?
You make the noise that makes it stop.
Lost. Cheek. Night. Speed.
Force the wheel in another direction.
Black. Muscle. Stars. Wind.

And there was death, too, of course, springing
out of the blackest ditch. The horse
was bred to run; its ankles
twitched for minutes. The boy
was seventeen; he woke
tasting metal, salt.

Black. Muscle. Stars. Wind.
A man dragged the horse away in pieces.
Black. Pulse. Strange. Light.
I swear, that's what the paper said.
Black. Crust. Oil. Shine.

A man dragged the horse
to the side of the road, stayed with the boy
until squad lights found them. "Weirdest thing,"
one EMT said, shaken, "someone else out there
in the middle of nowhere. And a flock
of starlings carrying on, just like it was daytime."

And the man, the man?
They want the rest,
want to know it has an ending.
Black. Wing. Song. Worm.
Black. Crust. Gravel. Gone.

A Breeze Finds a Curtain in a Half Open Window

TUESDAY: RHUBARB, LATTICE CRUST

Three things you can't control: life, death, and children. Lord knows, you've sure tried. Good God knows, there's holy risk just beyond the farm lane's bend. And the paper and the radio shout of doom-oh-doom-oh. Yet you *can* force certain things to taste as you expected; you can bake brave resolution into rhubarb, its stiff pink bowties cut off dangerous and fresh. Force the fever out; it just takes three cups of sugar and an unwatched boiling. Change what might have puckered into filling, feathery-sweet. You contain the lot with lattice: no escape, no wandering.

When the children were children, you fretted. And when stewing stopped, disasters! nearly happened. Yes remember the child falling down the hay hole in the barn loft (You gathering baby teeth on cement below)? Or the child running for your arms, into the gallop of a Morgan's muscled path (hooves ginger in mid-flight so that not one scratch ever surfaced)?

You still tremble at these awe-full almost-endings, have polished them for over 50 years. Even alchemy that turns a garden vegetable to fruit can't erase your puckered face squinting down into reflection—even with the cup of sugar that claims it's heaping-full. A slice of rhubarb pie: now that, for now, can carry the peace of your best measurements.

Service

Our *conchies* left farms to serve
in mental asylums, jumped from
planes to burning trees, did time
in Alcatraz, buried in uniforms by
force. But they could not stop The
War, could not live like other men,
still hear the silence of no parade.

The same couple's on the court-
house steps each Monday, holding
homemade banners: "War is Not
the Answer." Old, they are old,
have been doing this forever.
Their bodies, brief parentheses,
don't stop most passers-by.

Three towns away, a vet home
from a third Basrah tour hangs
a flag on the porch, upside-down.
Streets froth at noon, white water
river in front of him. No one stops
to ask him what he's done. He is
thinking of three faces, turning.

Material

The night before my baptism,
Satan preached as a rat
on my mother's kitchen table.
In that dream, children
gathered to listen, then
to watch me run.

You can't tell
that my people are plain
just by my father's surname. He converted
after Vietnam, married
the Amstutz daughter. She calls all caps
bonnets, her good eye
blue, the other winking hazel.

Barely moth wings found along a path:
the old widows' coverings in the very back
pew, the last of their roofed kind inside
the hometown sanctuary.

When they're gone, whose heads
will take their place? Burning
embers, the king's daughters. I am
showing you what I wear.

Figure 1.5 The full moon pulls out dreams like silk pajamas from open drawers. For weeks, my sleep's been filled with characters in plain dress, actors in bonnets or suspenders pretending to be something they're not. I am the one who calls them out, reveals their false identity. Exact accusations from these dreams: "Who's your bishop?," "What have you given up?," "What's your favorite cheese?" The question I get most often about my upbringing: "So what makes *you* different from *me*?" Sometimes, it also feels like accusation.

Figure 1.5a Last night, I was going to build a house on the edge of my grandpa's farm—but in the dream, I didn't recognize the land. I wake up frightened.

Dress Up

How easily I slip
inside her
wedding dress

bought for less than
five dollars
at the local thrift shop.

Dark sack, no pooled
silk—her love, like sin,
marked plain.

It could have been sewn
for my waist, my bust, only
its *Swartzie* bonnet

rimmed in lace.
A black tapestry to cover
her illuminated text

becomes my All Hallow's
costume. Lit
candles spiral

spirits on the living.
Our ancestors like her
hidden copper treasure:

unbraided, uncoiled past
her shoulders at night.
Wine leaves the glass.

I can forget what I'm wearing,
can un-name she who tied
the knots after needle,

shadow in my doorway
wanting her best dress
back.

Refurbished

They were always used for more
than just the herd and harvest. There
were rusting out trucks to shelter and when
the trains were still running, hobos
to house overnight; tobacco leaves to dry
if other crops brought in little, even
selves to hang, sometimes, from
those hand-cut oak beams. We used them

for advertising: chew and politicians, state
bi-centennials, peace signs during war. Quilts
painted on old pine siding, too: the Ohio Rose
or the Star of Alabama against the hushed green
of windrows, a field still used for a field. Only
once have I driven past an Amish church service
late on a summer morning, so close I could
make out a cadence in German, boys
swinging legs from benches laid out

where straw was just yesterday. As I drove away,
my lungs filled with something other, and I wanted
the world to go on, as is. Not all of the leaning
will be taken down to make photo frames, fruit crates,
Long Island mudrooms. Some of it will be
reborn standing, roofs patched, walls mended into
gallery, theater, B&B, homeless shelter, home.

We'll walk into a bookstore by the Pennsylvania
turnpike, knowing well and good what it's been before.

Icon

No one wants the family farm, or can
afford it until my only sister
imagines her three children
tucked in upstairs rooms or charging
the vast front lawn: maybe a future
pony, a movable coop, another
fort in the woods next to remnants
we built with the neighbor boys. Yet she's
quick to add, *We'd put up a crucifix,*
and the house would burst
into flames! I laugh with her

but try to see it too: Pope Francis
waving from a fridge photograph, air
perpetually stirred by the sign of
the cross, while outside buggies
climb the hill and neighbors hang out
plain clothes. For so long, I've given my sister
a soft and golden glow. Once,
we sang a line of hymn, and our voices bent,
just so, to reach each other.

But we're older now, old enough
that she warns me I may not be doing
my holy duty. I've converted
to other things. Each of her children
has almost taken her. She was brought

back to us once, days later, like some Rabbi
spotted outside her garden tomb. She tells me
all life is sacred, no special cases. I look hard
at her scars, the 159 miles between us
she hasn't traveled in half a decade. Now

I know my sister's children. I'm the auntie
who visits and takes communion only
twice a year, doesn't know the new prayers
said in unison. But Francis stares across
my kitchen, too, wreathed in painted sparrows
with tiny halos of their own. I don't claim him;
our eyes never meet. He's looking somewhere

in the distance, maybe a sun-warmed street
in Assisi or into the eyes of a wolf
or a bishop. He's never said anything to me
except for *Come: put down the weapon*
of your choice.

The Barn's Leper Face

MONDAY: PEACH

Once, there was a path from springhouse to kitchen's side entrance splitting the hill. Once, there was a sudden almost-funeral: daughter gasping in the water trough, pushed in by older brother-now-turned-senator. Farmers once retrieved dippers for clear gulps between harvest and the afternoon milking, the springhouse door fashioned to resist an Indian hatchet. Never has the ground renounced its bubbling over. Never has the orchard needed anything but "seconds" (fruit already dropped), to achieve reincarnation in aluminum tins. See? Collected bruises never tasted so good. The secret is to let split skins feel holy while bobbing in water called up from family land. Once, you lugged late peaches to the porch, cut all the good bits into bowl after bowl. The honeybees came, so you offered sloppy fingers, held them out for other mouths like you've done all this time. The barn's leper face, the best John Deere sold, the dinner bell silent, mostly. You held out.

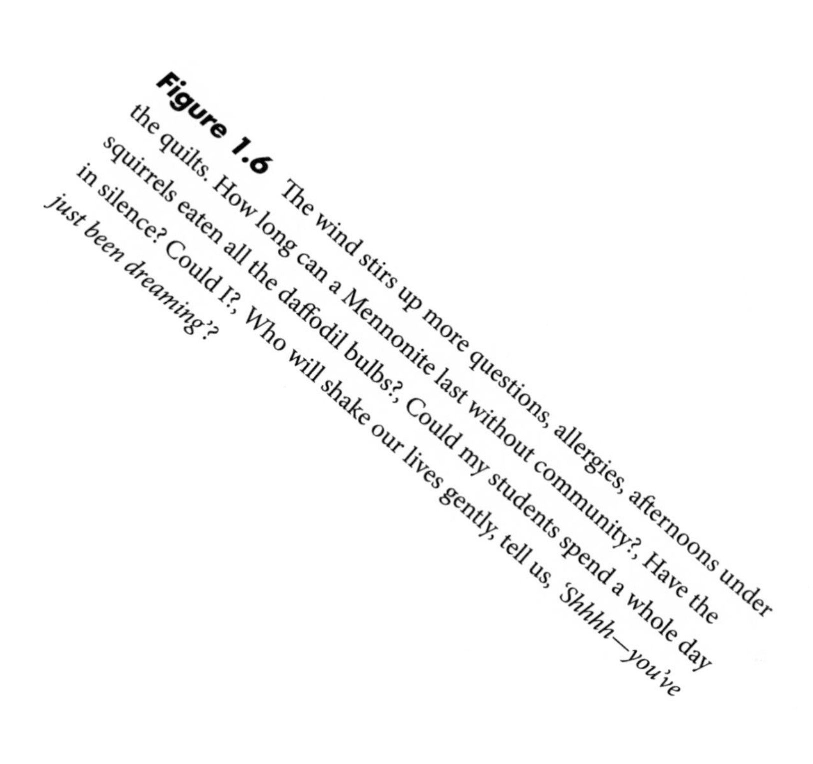

Figure 1.6 The wind stirs up more questions, allergies, afternoons under the quilts. How long can a Mennonite last without community?, Have the squirrels eaten all the daffodil bulbs?, Could my students spend a whole day in silence? Could I?, Who will shake our lives gently, tell us, *'Shhhh—you've just been dreaming'?*

Wait

—AFTER PSALM 27

I have seen things shine. Most days, this is enough:
    my escape route
more grace than gravel. Every stop-motion memory
of failure stocked in my body like grain.
    I am the harvest's vessel, full and waiting
for a match
to find fire where I stand, the whole mess
blitzing down. The heavens want me
    empty now. I open
my mouth and sing.

Mama said *Don't* as many times
    as she could. But my shield, in the end,
is gravity, the faith root not yet
weeded out.

Since childhood, it's been the same landlord
leaving me notes on the kitchen table he built
    into the hard wood floor. *This will someday be yours,*
he signs at the bottom. "This" is all
I've ever wanted—to stop
    being homesick,
to cry at the beautiful
    God looking out of a stranger, make my life
    from something sung
out of joy, not out of training.

There are deer in the gardens
again. And someone's name
    I don't recognize
all over the mail and magazines.

The landlord was once out of town
    for weeks. I asked for different light
bulbs. He brought
me lamps instead. I think it's him

who throws the fuse, switches off
    the news when I've been listening
for hours. Who needs that rabble,

    anyway? I do. I just want the headlines
to be different. *Me too,* he nods. *Me too.*

Schooling

At the Student Writing Center, she hands me
her conclusion. I am supposed to hone
the voice, make sense of jumbled syntax. I want,
instead, to know the name of the boy
in her oval locket, why she wears
the *hijab* and full-length dress so far
from Baghdad, at college now, how to make
that daily choice in favor of my own veiled
history. I try but cannot ask her.
Instead, we search for smooth transitions.
I tell her the language is already
beautiful, but it needs to stop in different places;
the meanings of phrases
aren't always what they seem. Though she wishes
I could, I just can't explain our rules
for everything. She grins as she's leaving,
squeezes my hand like our countries aren't still
at war. I watch her in the college green,
bright stem in the crowd, other students barely dressed
for summer. I am not her synonym.
I am no allusion.

Figure 1.7 Even Thoreau kept secrets hidden by the louder things he said, had his mother do his laundry. The wind blows our socks from the clothesline and into the woods. The president gives a speech. We forget what we're funding. It's too warm to care. I may never know what my students have learned from me.

In the Froth of Heaven's Whisking, Some Thing Takes Up Where You Left Off

WEDNESDAY: LEMON MERINGUE

It's taken sixty years of marriage, but your meringue technique is perfect; you could frenzy fresh egg whites into stiff peaks in your sleep. Two lemons, juiced and zested; cornstarch, salt, and margarine. Now no recipe is needed for your husband's favorite kind. You married in the summer when a storm drenched opened peonies around the tiny chapel. You still think of soft white petals when meringue is in the making, often say a prayer in silence as the pie slides onto rack: if you take it out—exactly—when its peaks are glazed with amber, you assume the role of Rescuer, suppose the plea's received intact. You . . . let the pie . . . cool.

St. Francis Holds Out Strawberries

Though he is the youngest,
he is ready. His sisters help run laundry
through the wringer in the basement, clear
the breakfast table, clean
straw and manure from the night's
still-warm eggs. His brothers' arms lift
feed, lead the draft horses to back fields,
fetch a neighbor's spare buggy horse, drag
a dead pig from the barn.

He carries his favorite kitten to the end
of the long lane, bare feet avoiding
puddles and caterpillars. And when
the first car weaves through the hills, slows
at the sight of him, its passengers wearing sunglasses
and pointing on their way to the cheese factory
or the auction barn, he takes a step toward
the road, holds a quart of bright berries above
his head with both hands.

Sometimes only the women get out,
and the car waits to move again, its doors hanging
open. His cheeks hurt from smiling. He has learned
to nod yes, no matter what he thinks they are
asking, to accept the soft bills right away. And even
when he tires of the kitten and the staring, starts
to cover his face when a car passes, he still uses

one hand to hold out what he is offering. He needs
no sign, and his work gets done without having
to speak a word.

Natural Horsemenship

Broom handles with paper
horse heads attached, up and down
asphalt at recess, our family farms long ago
emptied of livestock. I'd still learn
the smooth shell of a saddle, stalls
weighted with piss,
legs and hips adjusting to being
on land again. Decades later,
the ground percussion, a herd
of Spanish horses bolted toward me,

the beautiful creatures wanting
apples. All I could give them was fear

grown into a woman who lives out, in one way
or another, what it feels like to fall
from a full gallop, unable to pull back on
the reigns. I stood outside the fence
and let them sense it. Then I opened
the gate—it's what I had to give.

Always the Grandfathers

In my family, it's always the grandfathers
who come back from the dead, appear

to a widow in the half bath's cracked mirror
or stand in the driveway when she's backing

out the Buick. They come back but won't say
why, like the summer night Great-grandpa

Amstutz plodded down the farmhouse steps.
I watched his slow decent from the kitchen,

forgetting my midnight thirst. He walked while
buttoning coveralls for muck work in the barn;

I'd seen men do it hundreds of times. Five in the
morning, and no roosters alive to wake him.

I've talked to Grandpa Skeeter. He does not smell
like Lucky Strikes when we meet, his hair thick

waves of white since thirty. In dreams, he tells me
to get over myself; we're always waiting for food

on the grill or a parade to light uptown. Awake,
I don't remember his advice, can't string together

three words we said in confidence. Just the timbre
of his voice, a warm color in the back of my throat.

Still Craving When the Shell Is Empty

FRIDAY: PIQUANT SUBSTITUTION

The black walnuts' first drum stroke on the roof starts the annual crusade. Squirrels gather against Ohio's winter; we plunder for the possibility of pie, load our ten-gallon buckets, work gloves still stained from last year's harvest. All in the name of fudge or cookies, of salted handfuls in-between meals. It used to be that Ivan owned this battle, cracked heathen hulls with corn husker or hammer, spread oily kernels to dry for weeks in the garage. This year, vertigo; his body adjusts to new parts of the heart and brain's slow shunt. Long past chemo, post-80: time to settle into armchair nest, watch his first Christmas tree put into earth on Epiphany, its high green now taller than the attic. You set the oven to 450, set out all ingredients if he talks of pecan pie. And your daughter's family walks across the hay field, or your son drives in from Wooster at least two times a week. The table's solid walnut, one of Ivan's best old projects. Can't all fit around it now. Vanilla settles in the curtains. Squirrels scurry on the roof, nervous that we're there watching and warring. Pie still tastes the same.

St. Francis Considers His Own Advice after Finishing a Chaplaincy Shift at Mercy Memorial Hospital

If you have no voice after reading Rumi
to a dying man you hardly know, this is
a good and timely thing. *Pay attention.*

If you've sworn to stay at the hospital
for two days, end up staying ten, you
are the wind that rocks me forward.

There are lights in the city that never
know an off-switch or what it is they
illumine. *Be this*, you beg old friends,

your voice still husked in rattle after
the man's body has been rolled out and
you've left the book of poetry for night-

shift nurses to dog-ear, after you've followed
uncountable shoes across the salted
street, clamping onto the living

hands that let you feel two pulses meet.

Figure 1.8 Accepting the shape of one life takes practice. Remember asking for someone to help you trace the outline of your body on a sheet of torn-off paper? Did you recognize yourself as only border? I swear, just now, I smelled what the garden could be.

Moving the Mother

The morning our mother
church—dragged by pulleys,
hovering above cleared fields—begins
her months-long trek
across town   where she'll rest
                   as marker and altar, a welcome
                   center for tourists,
reminder of when scripture in High German
meant unity, and there wasn't much
                   permission
                   to want such scarring

                   change, I stand

with hands in pockets, blue scarf
shielding mouth from late
November's freeze.

In my family's north
acreage, I watch
the forced migration,
only a visitor.   The church, white ark
                   in the distance, crawls forward
                   another inch over
truck and tractor grinding,
men shouting, a bulldozer's
black-belch growl. Men moving

the mother, mostly men
paying for
her second life
to begin. No accident:

the blessing/half-warning
that streaks through my torso
as I turn to go back
to my own voice on paper: *Rest,*
you can't hurt us now, I say
to the mother, to the same
                                    floorboards where
                                    my great-great-great grandfather
                                    shuffled to his pew.

Can you forgive

a building? I tilt my head
toward this question   and lean into wind that's
taken one end of my scarf,   turning me into
a blue flare walking, my own mother one

field over, pacing her dining room,
preparing another sermon.

The Piano Tuner's Wife

Stringed instruments proffer
us most.

Muscle must
curve intervals—no gentleness

about it. He needs two solid arms, a dark-
welled ear to judge

frequency in
everything, even my voice

when it registers
in pleasure. His favorite need
and answer: the dissonant

aum

he can't bend into unison: a train
whistle passing below,   my last
name changed to his.

St. Francis Gives the Children's Sermon

The little glass house rang out
in song: cicadas joined us
on the second chorus of "All Creatures
of Our God and King," turning
the heads of flustered
choir members. A Monarch
pupa stirred, slippery
wings for the first
time considering sky outside
their Mason jar. Fluorescent
lights surged during
verse four with organ,
and old women with all
the old hymns memorized
clasped hands to laps,
unaware that the guest
tarantula went missing.
And even those whose bodies
never did bear any fruit,
the holy inside them, it ached
to get out, hang taut
as cello strings—a name
unspoken
and spoken above them.

Head of the Table

SATURDAY: ANIMATED CHERRY

Sometimes the dream gets muddled:
one night, it's barn swallows; another,
a gold rooster that flares up from double
crust when the first cooled piece gets cut.
Always, you're amazed that feathers come
out clean, survive the oven's fire: Abednegos
with wings. And it's your hands covered
in canned cherry filling. Right before
waking, it turns to red syrup—or blood
dried from that day's slaughter—or the
notyetbaby lost while picking apples.
But in this dream, the daughter lives and
the animals won't die. They're reborn into
pale eggshells, they break free from pie plate,
up from bubbling filling phoenix, and each
speaking things you later can't recall. All
you know is that the table's full: the hobo
John, the minister's wife, your children young
with school friends. They laugh and gape in
wonder, as if such unexpected guests were
what they'd wanted to be served all along.

Elsewhere

—DIA DE LOS MUERTOS, 2012

Ivan, if I could I'd move your ashes
to where you really wanted them: looking out
over valley and creek bed, waiting on train
whistle, the percussion of Old Order buggies
on the hill. You'd be a planted sapling in the spent

family orchard. If I had my way, you'd exhale
where the ground really knows you. Across the world
today, people talk to their dead, believe

they'll get an answer. It wasn't always so
far of a drive. I was once the grandkid living

one field over. Today, I'll bring you
bursts of wild mustard, eat the dirt-sweet
Queen Anne's root just like you showed me.
You'll have your own basket of mashed potatoes,
an angel food cake, hymn pages torn

straight from spine, their fluttering anchored.
I'll hire a cat to sleep
right above you, bring with it the cool

musk of the barn. When was the last time,
I wonder, that you stood in the hayloft to inhale

the generations? Five years, ten—has it been that long
since you shoved the stall doors open? Your death month
a black walnut fell across my metal roof. It only took
three men and a day to chainsaw its top-heavy canopy,
rig ropes, then lower spinning trunk

toward lawn, a slow ballet
that could kill a man. I watched
from inside, hands covering my mouth.

What was saved was also perfect, not one crack.
Four months later, it waits in heavy pieces

for my cue. And before I knew you'd also
change the landscape, I touched that trunk
like its weight was a whale
cast from ocean. What a waste
that your woodshop can't know this altar, that

the farm will be sold
outside the family—the reason, I'm guessing,
your ashes are elsewhere. But you know

I've done my leaving, am doing it now. I can
go, I can let go. A tree grows in both directions.

Notes

Though Mennonites and Amish share the same Anabaptist ancestry, the Amish broke away from the Mennonites in the 17th century. To this day, most American Amish live out a stricter faith and lifestyle than their American Mennonite neighbors. While my mother had to wear a head covering to church while growing up in an Old Mennonite community, I have never been asked to choose this physical symbol of my faith and culture.

Rumspringa refers to the period of time when Amish youth are encouraged to experience the outside world before joining the countercultural religious community for life. Even today, most will end up saying farewell to the "English," non-Amish world for good.

The nickname *Swartzie* in "Dress Up" refers to the Swartzentruber Amish, the most conservative Anabaptist group in Ohio.

"Latest Letter" is a found poem about Kidron, Ohio shaped from emails, letters, local newspaper clippings, and actual conversations.

"Moving the Mother" is inspired by Sonnenburg Old Mennonite Church, the first communally built meetinghouse in Kidron, Ohio, an early nineteenth-century Swiss-German settlement. This mother church would eventually break off into three separate churches built within a mile of each other. Congregational schisms happened over issues like speaking English, supporting adult education classes on Sundays, and differing views on women's public roles and dress. The original building, moved in 2013, now serves as a welcome center.

The pie poem series is loosely based on what I imagine to be the psyche of my Grandma Ruth, 85, who still starts many mornings by baking a pie to give away. Though she's known and loved for many things, this "pie ministry" is one of them.

Acknowledgments

Poems from this collection first appeared in the following publications, sometimes in altered forms:

Alimentum: The Literature of Food online (with videos by artists Melissa Haviland and David Colagiovanni): “Someone Calls from the Porch, a High Voice Answers,” “In the Froth of Heaven’s Whisking, Some Thing Takes Up Where You Left Off”

The Cresset: “St. Francis Works at the Columbus Zoo,” “Head of the Table”

Consequence Magazine: “All Day I Let the House”

Every River on Earth: Writing from Appalachian Ohio (anthology): “Tourist Brochure for Athens, Ohio”

Image: “Rumspringa,” “Twenty-four Crusts to Be Frozen,” “The Barn’s Leper Face,” “A Breeze Finds a Curtain in a Half Open Window,” “St. Francis Appears at the Scene of an Accident, Then Joins the Murmuration,” and “St. Francis Considers His Own Advice after Finishing a Chaplaincy Shift at Mercy Memorial Hospital”

The Mennonite Center for Writing’s Online Journal: “Let Me Feel, Dear Body. Let Me, At Least, Desire,” “Dress Up,” “Latest Letter”

On Being’s blog for American Public Media: “False Spring” (the collected figure poems)

Riverside Artist Gallery, Marietta OH: “Preparation” appeared in “Poetry in Art”, which showcased new visual work inspired by poems

Ruminate Magazine: “Wait” (finalist for the 2012 Janet B. McCabe Poetry Prize)

Saint Katherine Review: “Moving the Mother”

Swink Magazine: “The Piano Tuner’s Wife”

About the Author

Becca J.R. Lachman lives with her husband Michael in SE Ohio, where she's spent the last ten years teaching, tutoring, and writing for Ohio University. Also a musician, Becca's original choral works are available through Heritage Press. Other books by Becca include *The Apple Speaks* (Cascadia Publishing House) and *A Ritual to Read Together: Poems in Conversation with William Stafford* (editor, Woodley Press). Her poems and essays have most recently appeared in *So to Speak*, *Image*, *Brevity*, and the anthology *Mothering Mennonite* from Demeter Press. She wishes to thank Vermont Studio Center, the Colrain poetry manuscript conference, the Ohio Arts Council, Mennonite Arts Weekend, the Gold Wake family, and her classmates and mentors at the Bennington Writing Seminars for supporting this collection in various shiny ways. To find out more about Becca and her work, visit http://www.becca-jr-lachman.com/.

CPSIA information can be obtained at www.ICGtesting.com
Printed in the USA
LVOW12s1937270315

432366LV00004B/219/P